SOUL CLOTHES

~ REGINA D. JEMISON

Foreword by Rev. Stephen G. Marsh

Reflections of America Series

Modern History Press

Soul Clothes
Copyright (c) 2011 by Regina D. Jemison. All Rights Reserved.
From the Reflections of America Series.

Foreword by Rev. Stephen G. Marsh

Library of Congress Cataloging-in-Publication Data

Jemison, Regina D.
　Soul clothes / Regina D. Jemison ; foreword by Rev. Stephen G. Marsh.
　　　p. cm. -- (Reflections of America)
　ISBN 978-1-61599-095-5 (pbk. : alk. paper) -- ISBN 978-1-61599-096-2 (alk. paper)
　1. Social justice--Poetry. I. Title.
　PS3610.E47S68 2011
　811'.6--dc22
　　　　　　　　　　　　　　　　　　2011017464

Published by
Modern History Press, an imprint of Loving Healing Press
5145 Pontiac Trail
Ann Arbor, MI 48105

www.ModernHistoryPress.com
FAX 734-663-6861
Tollfree 888-761-6268

Distributed by
Ingram Book Group, Bertram's Books (UK)

Dedication

For V. Christine Jemison and Ralph Jemison Jr.

Thank you for my life, the gift of living life, and choosing life over and over again.

Acknowledgements

So much to be grateful for...

To God for His bottomless grace for me!

To all my teachers of life and faith—Ma and Daddy who are watching over me. The seeds you planted are still growing and guiding me. I miss you more than words *as vast as the universe and numerous as grains of sand* can compute. Thank you for all the love and all the lessons.

To Pastor Carla Nelson for your teaching of scriptures that molded my thinking and my life. To Pastor Christine Thompson for giving nourishment and revelation to my voice of prayer and gift of ministry in the midst of a bone dry wilderness. To Pastor James C. Perkins for the gift of being in the presence of a master word smith of the Master and knowing you as my personal shepherd.

To Stephen G. Marsh for returning my muse and making this possible.

To Sherry Quan Lee for your keen listening, patient heart, and thoughtful spirit that helped to fulfill my dream.

To Khabira M.D. Raheem for healthy living, and most of all for a life well spent, yet is just beginning. Here's to an endless number of 13's!

Contents

Foreword by Rev. Stephen G. Marsh	iii
God Gave Me Words	1
Writin' My Blues Away	3
Because a door in my soul opens	5
Hold on to God, a lawyer's prayer	7
Welcome to Amerika	10
Today I Said a Prayer	12
Soul Clothes	15
WOMEN WAITING: breast cancer, a story	16
Lover, I Can't Make You	20
Soul Clothes	23
Embezzled Love from My Deposit Box of Protection	25
Divine Reflections	29
Kairos: past disappointment and down the street from ecstasy	30
Rocks of Remembrance: ancestral spirits and timeless wisdom	31
So Beautiful Just to Die	32
About the Author	33

Foreword

You are holding in your hands an engraved and personal invitation to enter into a literary as well as personal relationship with the deeply insightful and profoundly expressive perspectives of one of God's own trombones. As you encounter these soul-stirring pieces, the poetry, prose and personality of Regina Diane Jemison is likely to rub up on a curious and compassionate place within you, a place of stark reality drenched in divine hope. Imagine a John Coltrane solo, with words instead of tenor sax.

That's in part because Regina D. Jemison believes her life mission is to empower and prepare people to be their divine self at all times and under any and all circumstances. Needless to say, with such a seemingly impossible purpose, she relies on God in new ways every day. It was something she has been taught and led to do all her life.

As a young adult Christian, Regina began to get in touch with her vast spiritual gifts, which included her voice and vision for the divine possibilities of Black people in general, and the Black church in particular. She was anointed a Deacon in the Detroit Lutheran Coalition, itself an urban representative of the Evangelical Lutheran Church in America. In that role and many other spiritual accountabilities, she has been blessed to study under and provide sustenance and pastoral care for many eminent pastors, preachers and teachers of theological praxis. She serves the Spirit of the Living God through a multi-denominational ministry of service that finds its expression on national, local and individual levels.

The power and destiny of Spirit has molded all of the above – and more – into a powerful and cultural female voice of joy, outrage, love, anger, faith, challenge, surrender, healing and hope. A *searing* and *incisive* voice when it comes to the injustices God's people suffer on every level, because of *"isms"* of every kind. A *sacred* voice that cries out in the wilderness. A *compassionate* voice that cries out to Jesus. A *hopeful* voice that speaks of new life from old traditions. A *wise* voice that speaks of the laws of the universe. A *faithful* voice that speaks of a faithful God.

Those who have ears to hear, listen to what the Master of the universe is pouring through this blessed and highly favored lover and gift-bearer of written and spoken word, Regina Diane Jemison.

The Rev. Stephen G. Marsh

God Gave Me Words

cocoa and caramel and chocolate

Writin' My Blues Away

I.

I've been busy chasin'
chasin' children
        chasin' money
                chasin' men

No time to write
my blues away; chasin'

gave me the blues

chasin'
   seekin',
      workin',
         meanderin'

No time to write
my blues away

II.

But today
I see my beauty
      today I see my brilliance
           today God gave me

words that dance
      twistin' and shoutin'
      the blues away

My voice leaps on the page where joy
was lost and sorrow was at home, but

my soul
        wants to write
the blues away

the words
                                  are endless

III.

I'm writin' my prayers
    on stone tablets
        legal pads
            and blue skies, writin' the blues
away, writin'

    to trust
    to survive
    to influence
    to forgive

Because a door in my soul opens

I write

because it relieves
my sub-conscious feelings and
conscious thoughts,
my emotional baggage,
distorted delusions,
and my anger

writing illuminates injustice
gives language to people's pain
pictures to failing dreams

I write

to articulate
  my madness,
  my peculiarity,
    my wounds of disappointment,
my tears

exhausted
  elated
    or bewildered

I write

because a door in my soul opens
giving sustenance to my existence
a name to my feelings
breath to my spirit
  permanence to my world

I write

because the ups I can hide,
the downs I can overcome

I write

        piercing resignation
        electrifying your psyche
        reminding us who God is

I write
    alleviating the anger
I write
    rearranging the ramblings of my mind, while
    ordering the abundance of my heart
I write
    sentences that sink deep into the chasms of social inequities
I write
    paragraphs of prayers
I write
    phrases that transcend my illusions
    and give truth to my transgressions
I write
    allegories that artistically express my sexuality
    and my politics
I write
    syllables that give beauty to a starving life
I write
    homage to my friends and family

I write

    gaining entry
    into a world of healing compositions,
        poetic wholeness,
            and rooms of divine reflections

I write
and a door opens.

Hold on to God, a lawyer's prayer

My faith tells me that vengeance is not mine
My heart tells me we cannot wallow forever

Civil rights activists told me to fight the battle

> They didn't tell me
> I'd be weary, exhausted, disgusted, betrayed, disenchanted

Civil rights activists told me

> liberate, inspire, vindicate, evoke
> one day, one soul, one case, one love at a time

>> They didn't tell me
>> I'd be disillusioned, disappointed, and wounded

Ancestors told me

> God would not leave me, or forsake me
> when colleagues and clients abandoned their hearts

> God would give me tools and resources
> to get me through

>> Ancestors didn't tell me

>> I'd feel powerless, lose faith, despair, and grieve
>> my vision cloudy from all my tears

Disenchantment wasn't written in my textbooks:
Black's Law Dictionary or *Rules of Civil Procedure*

I didn't hear *exhaustion, disgust, betrayal* in a lecture

We didn't discuss *disappointment* in our discussion groups
    or over coffee or during office hours

No one said: *the rules would change, the legislators didn't care,*
    equality was theory

Reality wasn't in my law school welcome packet,
    the instruction manual,
        or test booklet

No one said: *freedom wasn't real, lives would be lost, babies*
    would be hungry

Reality wasn't mentioned at orientation,
    ordination,
        graduation
            or the swearing in ceremony

No one was saying: *violence was routine, shelter was optional,*
    hope would disappear

Answers didn't come with my state lawyer's license.

    I am angry. Pray less. Cuss more. Have scars. Shout louder.

Ancestors hold me, they told me

    Assurance comes in the twinkle of grandma's eye
      and the cushion on grandpa's knee
    Renewal comes in sermonic melodies of my pastors
      and the photographic memories of my aunts

    My mother loved and adored all that I was, I was not,
      and I am
    My father asked about my work & my life daily
      as if it was the first time, every time

I know my history
    I know my ancestors did not give up
        I know how hard my ancestors toiled

I search for intellectual reason and professional purpose
I seek emotional stability

    and spiritual revolution
    (even for a day)

My ego and hurt feelings tell me not to give up

    go on, be comforted, know your gifts, have faith…

I am listening.

Welcome to Amerika

to white men entering Amerika's penal system

I've always believed a white man can do anything and be anyone in
this country of white privilege—

I see it in the images,
economics,
politics, and
        psyche of this country ev-ver-ry-day. Yep, that's right. And,

> *I've always known Black men*
> *to be perceived*
> *to be powerless*
> *in a white power-filled country*

Well welcome to today,
the judge is black and doesn't look like u.
Do u question
the judge's harsh ruling
wondering if it is racially motivated

> *true or false:*
> *presumed innocent until proven guilty?*

I am saying, the thieves/the legislators
make mandatory minimum sentences,
while paying minimum wages
to court appointed attorneys
who work the max for the minimum
so u get maximum prison time
while doing time on your mandatory minimum. Damn.

> *this country's system,*
> *my system*
> *reeks of injustice and greed,*
> *devours life.*
> *is it color blind?*

Are u afraid?   Are u afraid?   Are u afraid?

Are you shocked! that you have been caught and penalized
for what you say is nothing but a minor crime?

>   *fear: felon, criminal, conviction, violence, and maybe death*

your freedom squelched, opportunities lost. Your working class
money
not enough to buy u options
    and Cochran
        and freedom, and Budzyn & Nevers
            and freedom,
                and Simpson and freedom,
                    and _____ and freedom,
                        and Donahue & Brown and freed—

Welcome to the Amerika Black people have always known. The one
    Mumia knows and
        Assata and
            Roger and Darnell,
                the one Malcolm and Martin knew,
                    the country Chokwe, Frederick, and Steven knew
                    the one Sundiata and Jalil and
                    the one my neighbor's son knows
the same one my brother James knows and my cousins knew,
                the Amerika the Panther 21, the Chicago 7,
                and the Cuban 5 knew,
                that same one,
                the same one

built on the blood, free labor, breast milk, and grit
of the oppressed,

>   *my people*

I am an Amerikan lawyer of African descent, welcome to my
Amerika.

Today I Said a Prayer

For my cousin Darnell E. Phifer
Sunrise, March 9, 1960
Sunset, December 21, 1996

Today I said a prayer
and cried for you

> For your suffering and limitations
> For perseverance and distress
> For the sores on your skin that made scabs on your heart
> For your days of medication and unknown side glances
> For your pain and the *good* bad days

Today I said a prayer
and
cried for you

> For those who rejected you
>
> > Who failed to remember your dance,
> > Your laughter, your physique, your style
> >
> > Who could no longer lick fingers full of your tasty cooking
> > Be informed or comforted by your wisdom
> > Hear your chuckle
> > Or see the light in your eyes

Today I said a prayer

> For *Don't Ask Don't Tell*
>
> > That carved secrets in your service
> > Casted shame on your friendships
> > and disgrace on your love

Today I said a prayer
and cried for us

> In memory of *exuberance and joy*
> *bid whist lessons,*
> *all night parties,*
> *and waking up the sun with laughter and good wine*
>
> *and dancing, walking, talking, laughing, smiling,*
> *and hugging*

Today I said a prayer
and cried

> For the world
> for babies and men
> mothers and women
> for epidemics and secrets,
> for your illness, the disease AIDS

I can't hug you.

Today,
I prayed and cried for me.

Soul Clothes

*You wear my purple turtleneck sweater
made of wool*

WOMEN WAITING: breast cancer, a story

My time is passing
Without regret
With struggle
Without love
With passion
My time is filled with purpose
intensity and passion
(Without glory and recognition)
My time is passing
full of hope, promise, and direction

I. Once upon a time: SILENCE

Women sat waiting
        patiently

with shooting throbbing pounding pain
radiating in the cavities of their breasts
and minds

Once upon a time

Disfigured by silence
Maimed by complacency
We were quietly vanishing
No one talked
        to share comfort, commonality, and fear

Once upon a time

there was no awareness
        no commercials, infomercials, or psa's
        no month set aside, or money for research
        no pink ribbons
        no marches or walks

Once upon a time

there were no reminders
        no hanging shower cards
        no breast self-examinations
        no informational pamphlets

Once upon a time

Women suffered in a cultural, physiological, sexual void
asking *why?*
generations of women and mothers and daughters
alone and afraid

Women, faded away, disappeared
into blinding fluorescent lights
of diagnostic rooms, x-ray rooms, waiting rooms

breasts lopped off

II. BREASTS

Symbols of growth/from child to teen to woman
Symbols of power/perky inviting nipples, sexy valley deep cleavage
Symbols of wealth/silicone valley for the rich
Symbols of burden/heavy, harnessed breasts in bondage bras
        causing shoulder scars and bent over back aches
Small breasts, symbols of inadequacies.

    fairy tales and myths

Eyes hollow, shoulders shrugged, hesitant hugs
would anyone know, if our breasts were gone?

Would anyone know the wrenching pain
in the cubby hole of our armpits
the inability to lift our arms or our voices?
Would anyone know our loss in the attic of our emotions?
Would anyone know the hole in our heart
the rejection of lovers, the confusion of husbands, the dismissal of
partners?

Would anyone know the humiliation in locker rooms, public restrooms, and airports?

III. Once upon a time: my story

I am the Woman waiting

for the results of my second mammogram and
bilateral ultrasound at Sinai Grace in Detroit, Michigan
waiting with women
old enough to be my mother or grandmother
they don't look like me, but

our breasts are gone

Once upon a time, not so very long ago,
I shopped for prosthesis,
prosthesis that didn't come in my size or shape or my brown color

> *prosthesis, the word doesn't even sound natural,*
> *doesn't sound like me*

foreign like the scar it was supposed to cover
or the facade it was supposed to create
so I wouldn't remember
the scars, the scars that I was afraid to touch, afraid
touching would make the absence of my breasts real

scars that debilitated my self esteem
ignited my anger
confused me
reminded me of the
cold detached treatment of doctors and nurses
        medical professionals turned insurance pimps

IV. Once upon time, today

Women speak CANCER
we look it in the eye, know and dismantle facts from myth and
share our knowledge, demand honesty and respect
straighten our backs, lift our songs

grieve
rejoice
live!

Lover, I Can't Make You

when we were young the elders told us, never say "i can't"

i can't make u love me,
        Black Man, lover
i can't make u love the color of my brown skin

i can't make you care about us
i can't make you do right by us
    can't make you hold your head high
    can't make you tell the truth
    can't make you remember who you are,
Black Man, lover, remember

        your integrity
        your truth
        your ancestral memory
        your fortitude
        your health
        your spirit
        your priorities
        your emotions
        your choice
        your free will
        your options and alternatives
        your own accounting
        your own discounting
        your beliefs
        your disbeliefs
        your suspicions

        your trust

        your power
        your capacity

i can't make u love you, Black man, lover,
i can't make u go to the doctor
i can't make u get tested
i can't make you fix our broken house or our broken spirits
i can't make you care about you

i can't make u stop or start, move forward or back
i can't make u turn away or turn up the intensity
i can't make u turn the corner or turn and run for you life
i can't make you be still

every time i want u
    not to use those drugs, engage that addiction,
    disappear for days
every time I want u
    not to destroy yourself, not forget who you are
    not to be strangled by a past that is long ago over
every time I want u not to leave
    i can't make u
every time i want u to call
    i can't make u
every time i want u to know you are greater than life's circumstances
    i can't make u
every time I want u to care about you, care about others,
every time I want you to care about life, and your calling in life
    i can't make u
every time i want u to say no
    i can't make u
every time I want u to scream *YES, I CAN*!
    i can't make u
every time i need u to be here with me
    i can't make u
every time I pray for your healing,
every time I pray for us to be together
every time I pray not to be disappointed
    i can't make u

every time i want u to trust me
    i can't make u

each time i want your forgiveness
    either u will or u won't
each time i want u to want me
    either u do or u don't
each time i want u to be healthy
    either u will or u won't
each time i want you to commit to our relationship
    either you do or u don't

each time I want the best for us
      either it will be or it won't

no amount of talking, coercing, cajoling or pleading
no amount or reasoning, rationalizing, or re-making
no amount of justification, substantiation or validation

u have made up your mind

determined your course
focused on your journey
fixed your mentality
resolved your indecision
established your position
u can

and so can i

and i have decided
i can't

i can't change u, and u can't change me; I am

caring
loving
sensitive
hardworking
vulnerable
afraid, and
      stubborn

u are who u are
    at peace or not
    healthy or not
    free or not
    loved or not
    affirmed or not
    on task or not

I am a woman wanting freedom
    either you want to be free or
        not.

Soul Clothes

I wear your hat
heavy, hip
it covers my ears and strokes my locks
I'm stylin'
I feel good in your hat your emotions intact
You feel good in my head

   jazz horns, happy faces, musical notes and big bootied women

I wear your favorite black t-shirt
cool, cotton lets me breathe
comfortable, my security blanket
soaking up the sweat of my obsession
I inhale the musk of you
exhale my shyness
I wash it and it doesn't shrink
I wear it until it stands on its own

   jazz horns, happy faces, musical notes and big bootied women

I wear your khaki shorts
wrinkled, roomy, unadorned
they sag, gaping in all the right places
pleated with predestined plans
your intricacies and idiosyncrasies
fit me

   jazz horns, happy faces, musical notes and big bootied women

You wear my purple turtleneck sweater
made of wool
looped with love, laughter, and laziness
the lines of your heart
wrapped up
wrapped around
weaved through me
my purple sweater
on your brown back
caressing your strength, honoring your accomplishments,
and warming your burdens

> *jazz horns, happy faces, musical notes and big bootied women*

big and strong, wearing
my desire

> *jazz horns, happy faces, musical notes and big bootied women*

i wear the fabric of your spirit
> *jazz horns, happy faces, musical notes and big bootied women*

it fits well
keeps me toasty
protects me from the draft of my fears
fondles my neck, my stomach, my thighs

> *jazz horns, happy faces, musical notes and big bootied women*

the fabric of my soul
the texture of you

> *jazz horns, happy faces, musical notes and big bootied women*

we wear cotton and wool together

Embezzled Love from My Deposit Box of Protection

No comfort in my voice, no lyrics in my song.
Stuck on one flat note.
God is real. People are crazy. Life is unpredictable. Love is solace.

My heart is overwhelmed by you,

discombobulated

my heart is overcome by you
       consumed, occupied, single tracked, over run
     at times
           betraying my focus
                losing my temper

missing my exit to church, forgetting my lunch, leaving my purse,
not getting to the point of my conversation, ranting nonsense,
raging insults, replacing my very thoughts

thinking of you, imagining being with you

      What are you doing?
What are you wearing?
    How do you feel?
        What are you saying?
    How is your soul today?

discombobulated

Contemplating
     the very essence of you
  what will make your spirit sing a new song
    your heart skip a beat
       your soul smile and your step skip in sheer elation?

Memory: the last time we kissed, the first time
we played chess, six hours reading to each other by candlelight

I spend my time wondering
       hoping, waiting, wanting
with disturbed thought and secret passion

I am angry you are here and I am there.

I want to touch you, smell you, hear your voice, wax philosophical

discombobulated

Overwhelmed
       my vision blurs
       the hairs on my legs grow

            I search for you

What are you doing?
       What are you wearing?
How do you feel?
   What are you saying?
     How is your soul today?

> *Are you reading the Bible, holding a friend's hand, singing, playin' the trombone, watching cartoons?*
> *Consciously counting money, guiltily counting women?*
> *Are you wearing baggy pants, a suit, a sweat suit —the armor of God?*

Discombobulated.

    You have taken over my consciousness,
    changed my goals,
    excited my sleeping senses,
    renewed forgotten and lazy instincts,
     inspired unknown voids and transcended psychological walls

Are you the salve for a cracked heart,
the balm for scars of old? The goodbye to *tired, unappreciated, guilt, addiction, and resentment?*

Yes!

I find myself full of you, your desires and possibilities

What are you doing?
What are you wearing?
How do you feel?
What are you saying?
How is your soul today?

Time passes
      desire rotates to the point of redundancy
  you/your love
          ruminating in my mind

    consider my love
    celebrate my being
    care for my soul
    educate my mind
    inspire

I have
      accepted my fate, no longer hesitate

You are
    the answer for my purpose, the rhythm for my work,
    the music for my muse, and the balance for my body.

I am
home.

Divine Reflections

My faith tells me that vengeance is not mine
My heart tells me we cannot wallow forever

Kairos: past disappointment and down the street from ecstasy

> *Inspired by Stephen G. Marsh who said: "In your writing describe places where you don't physically live but that you have been or want to go."*

Before heaven, and glorious.
It is a mountain as well as the valley beneath it.

I have seen it, my legs dangle off the edge.

I'm feeling like a kid again
  swinging my toes, unrestrained, teetering, looking down to possibilities.
Water falls like electric waves tickling the mind,
  soothing and calm.

I talk to merchants trading books of wisdom,
I hear music: drums beating and elders chanting
I see art : ancient symbols, bright colors, and a Joshua tree

Healing and Emancipation.

I taste cocoa and caramel and chocolate
and sweet potatoes
I drink teas, roots, and wines

The water is clear, food vibrant

No money will do
Courage and choice paves the way
Come swim, walk or fly

Smell the frankincense and valerian
See indigo

Rocks of Remembrance: ancestral spirits and timeless wisdom

water, sweet nectar, water

Water, sweet nectar, the heart of God
Sweetens my life and heals my spirit
Washes away my sins and my shortcomings
Fills the empty tomb of my soul

Sweet nectar
Nurtures the hills and the valleys
Feeds creatures on belly, wing, or foot
Sweet nectar from heaven

Praise God! Sweet nectar
Rips through my sadness
Over rocks of remembrance
I remember stones removed, pain relieved, life anew

Water reshaped my perspective, cleared my senses, gave me spirit

Sweet nectar, fragrant, full of promise
Altering time, creating unity
Now and forevermore – unceasing
Glistening and glimmering
Reflecting ancestral spirits and timeless wisdom

Sweet nectar
The tears in your eyes
The sweat of your brow
The radiance of your skin and the sparkle of your smile
Sweet nectar, we grow with grace and strength
Our minds saturated, love from the heart of God

Water flows, then and again, and again
God's righteousness
Sweet nectar, abides in our bodies, 60-70% of our very being
Water surging, moving, gushing, through every cell, through heartache. Water over rocks.

So Beautiful Just to Die

A flower was born, and so was I

      into a world already turning
      into a universe already on course
    life predestined

to be beautiful
and flourish amongst others
different beginnings
same beauty

diversity/community

      chrysanthemums
                petunias
         lilies
  ivies
      yuccas
                  gladiolas
    begonias
          sun flowers
  and birds of paradise

are creative, and nurture until seasons change
and petals shed

and, then

we are born again.

About the Author

Regina was born and raised in Detroit, Michigan and educated in the Detroit Public School System, graduating from Cass Tech High School. She then obtained a Bachelor of Business Administration from the University of Michigan, and a Juris Doctorate from Wayne State University. She has researched, practiced and taught law and law enforcement since 1993 in various undergraduate and graduate levels. She has owned her own law practice since 1995. She has also been the Legal Instructor at the Detroit Police Academy. In both her life and law practice, Regina is a tireless advocate, motivational presence, drum major for justice, and intimate intercessory prayer warrior. She is also a compassionate companion of those who are chronically ill, as well as those who are transitioning from this life to the next.

Please visit www.ReginaJemison.com

THE REFLECTIONS OF AMERICA SERIES
"What one person makes possible becomes possible for all people"

Soul Clothes
by Regina D. Jemison

Tales of Addiction and Inspiration for Recovery:
Twenty True Stories from the Soul
by Barbara Sinor, PhD

Saffron Dreams
by Shaila Abdullah

Confessions of a Trauma Junkie: My Life as a Nurse Paramedic
by Sherry Jones Mayo

My Dirty Little Secrets--Steroids, Alcohol, and God
by Tony Mandarich

The Stories of Devil-Girl
by Anya Achtenberg

How to Write a Suicide Note:
serial essays that saved a woman's life
by Sherry Quan Lee

Chinese Blackbird
by Sherry Quan Lee

Modern History Press

www.ingramcontent.com/pod-product-compliance
Lightning Source LLC
Chambersburg PA
CBHW061310040426
42444CB00010B/2581

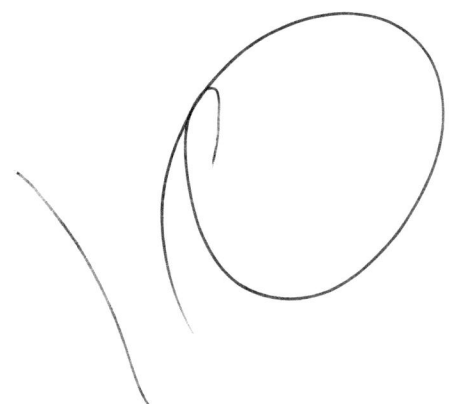

Observations sur les rapports présentés au roi et aux deux chambres et sur les budgets de 1815 (Éd.1814)

Formé